A Gift For

Laura

From

Shannon

Published by Gift Books from Hallmark,
a division of Hallmark Cards, Inc.,
Kansas City, MO 64141

Visit us on the Web at www.hallmark.com.

Editorial Director: Todd Hafer
Editor: Theresa Trinder
Art Director: Kevin Swanson
Designer: Mary Eakin
Production Artist: Dan Horton

Printed in the U.S.A.
ISBN: 978-1-59530-145-1
BOK4323

Girl Talk

Telling It Like It Is

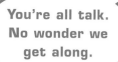

Girl Talk

Telling It Like It Is

Sometimes
IT TAKES TEAMWORK
TO PULL A GUY'S HEAD
OUT OF HIS BUTT.

~

God Gave It,
BUT YOU GOTTA SHAKE IT.

~

There Are Two Things
THAT NEVER GO OUT OF STYLE:
SELF-CONFIDENCE AND
THE LITTLE BLACK SHOE.

~

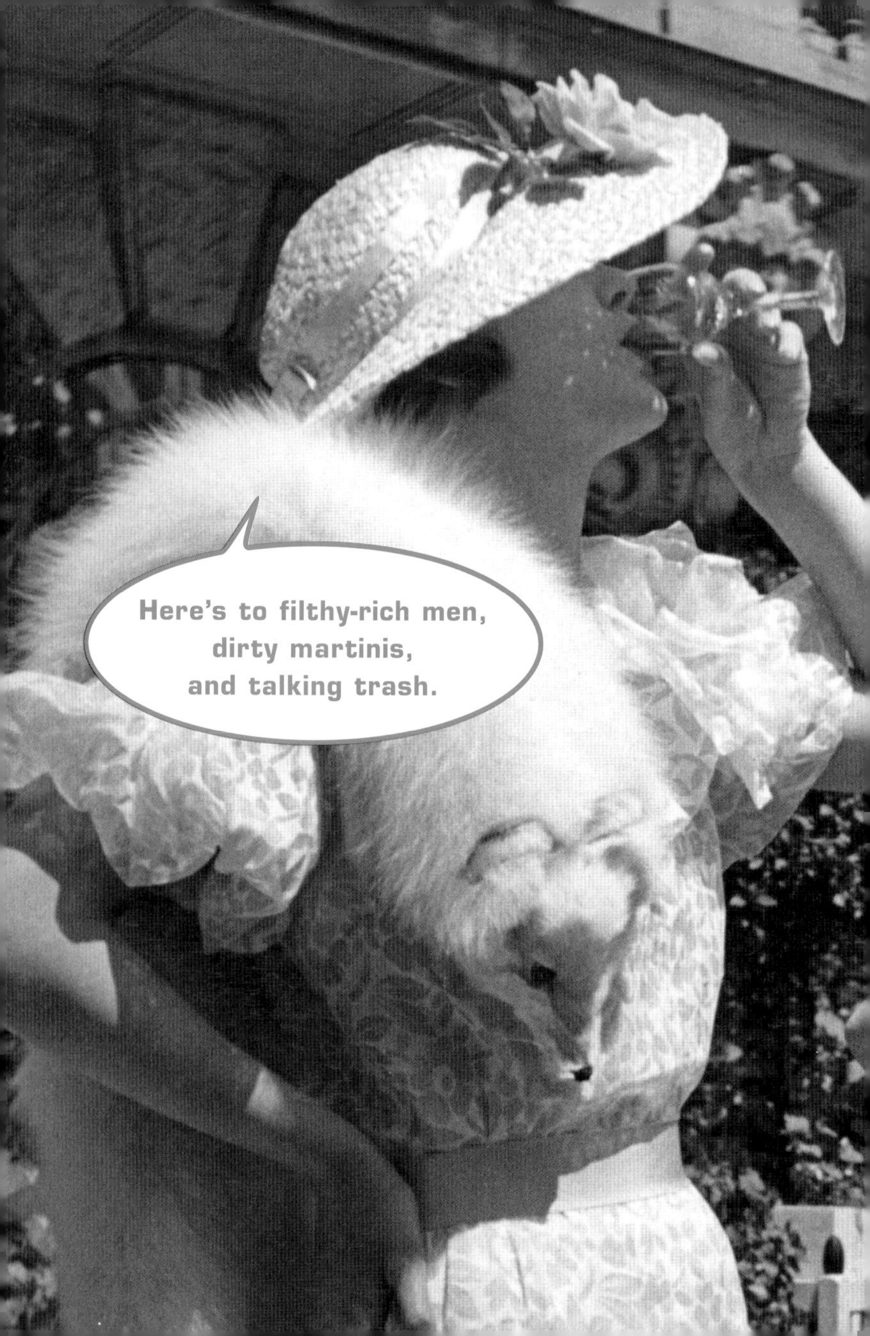
Here's to filthy-rich men, dirty martinis, and talking trash.

Women
KNOW HOW TO AVOID
HAVING SOME GOOD,
CLEAN FUN.

~

The Glass Ceiling
WOULD BE NO MATCH FOR THE DETERMINED JOHNSON TWINS.

~

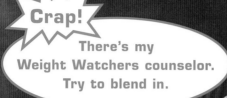

Gossip
AT THE GARDEN CLUB
~

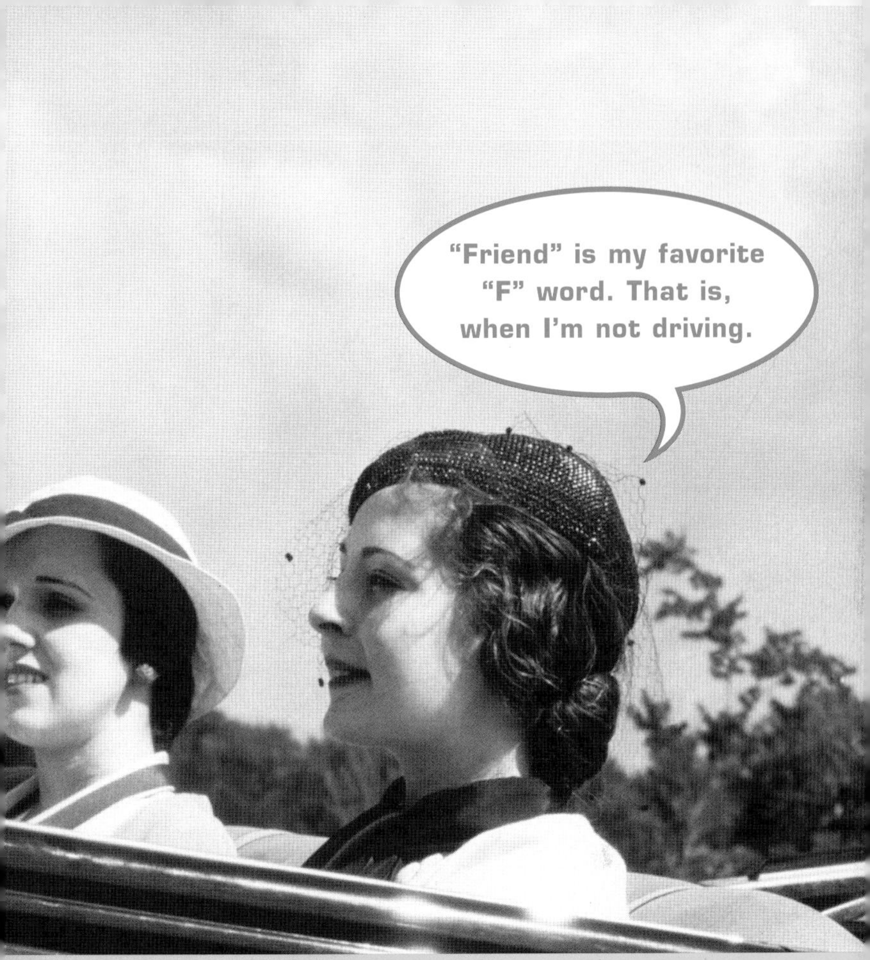
"Friend" is my favorite "F" word. That is, when I'm not driving.

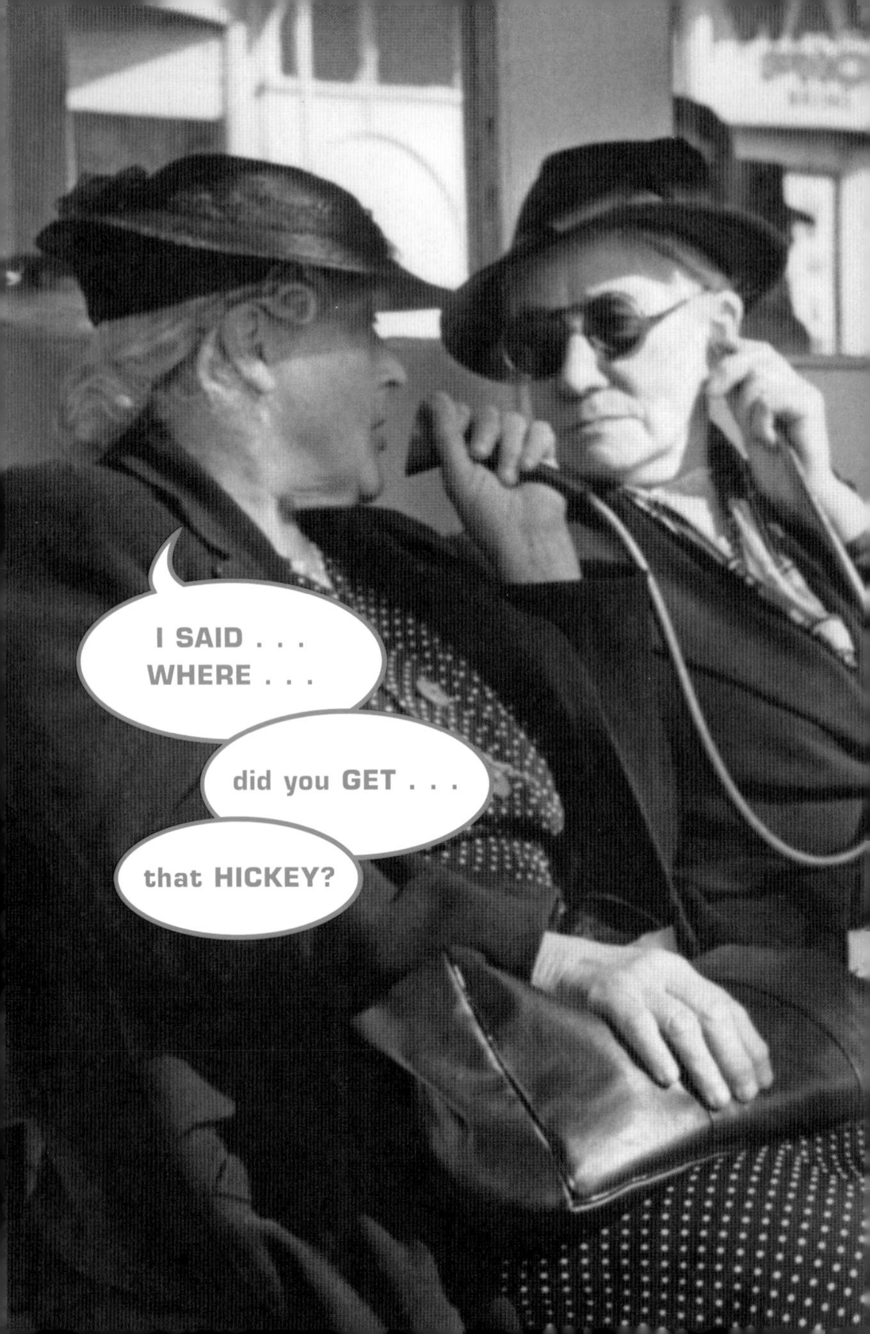
I SAID . . .
WHERE . . .
did you GET . . .
that HICKEY?

He asked for a warm-up, so I said, "Sure. And then would you like some more coffee?"

Humor
AND FRIENDSHIP—
THE KEYS TO A WORKING
WOMAN'S SURVIVAL.

~

Hell Hath No Fury
LIKE A WOMAN WHO DOESN'T LIKE
YOUR TONE OF VOICE.

~

There's
NOTHING BETTER
THAN SITTING DOWN
WITH A GOOD FRIEND
OVER A GOOD CUP
OF COFFEE. PLUS
IT HELPS YOU SOBER
UP AFTER BOOK CLUB.

~

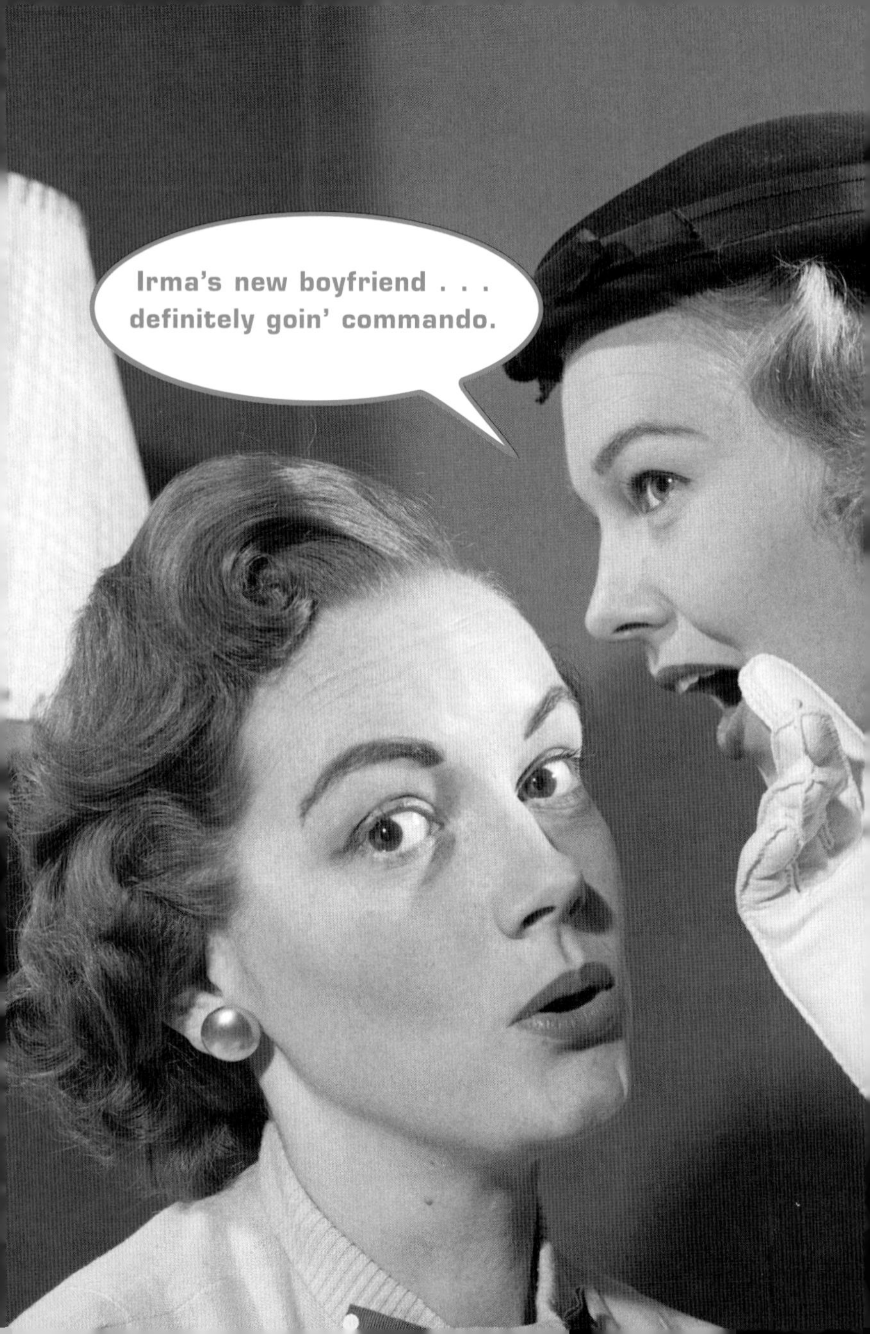
Irma's new boyfriend . . . definitely goin' commando.

It's Important
TO NOTICE THE LITTLE
THINGS IN LIFE.

~

Sometimes the Line
BETWEEN HIGH FASHION
AND "WHAT THE HELL HAPPENED?"
CAN GET A LITTLE BLURRY.

~

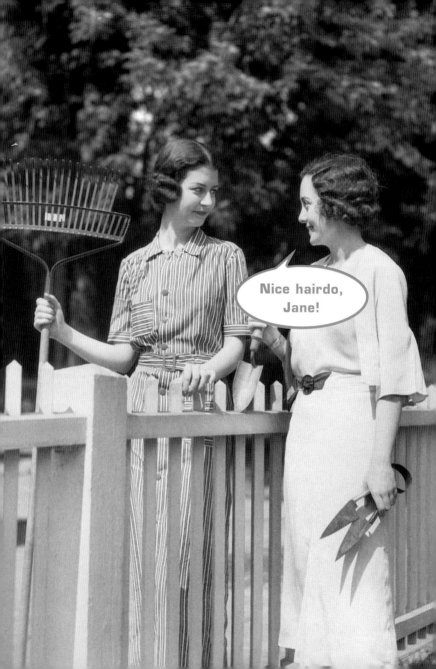

A Good Tight Set
OF BUNS WILL NEVER
GO UNAPPRECIATED.

~

Sometimes
BEFORE A DATE,
PAM AND BOBBI LIKE
TO PRACTICE LOOKING
AS IF THEY GIVE A DAMN.

~

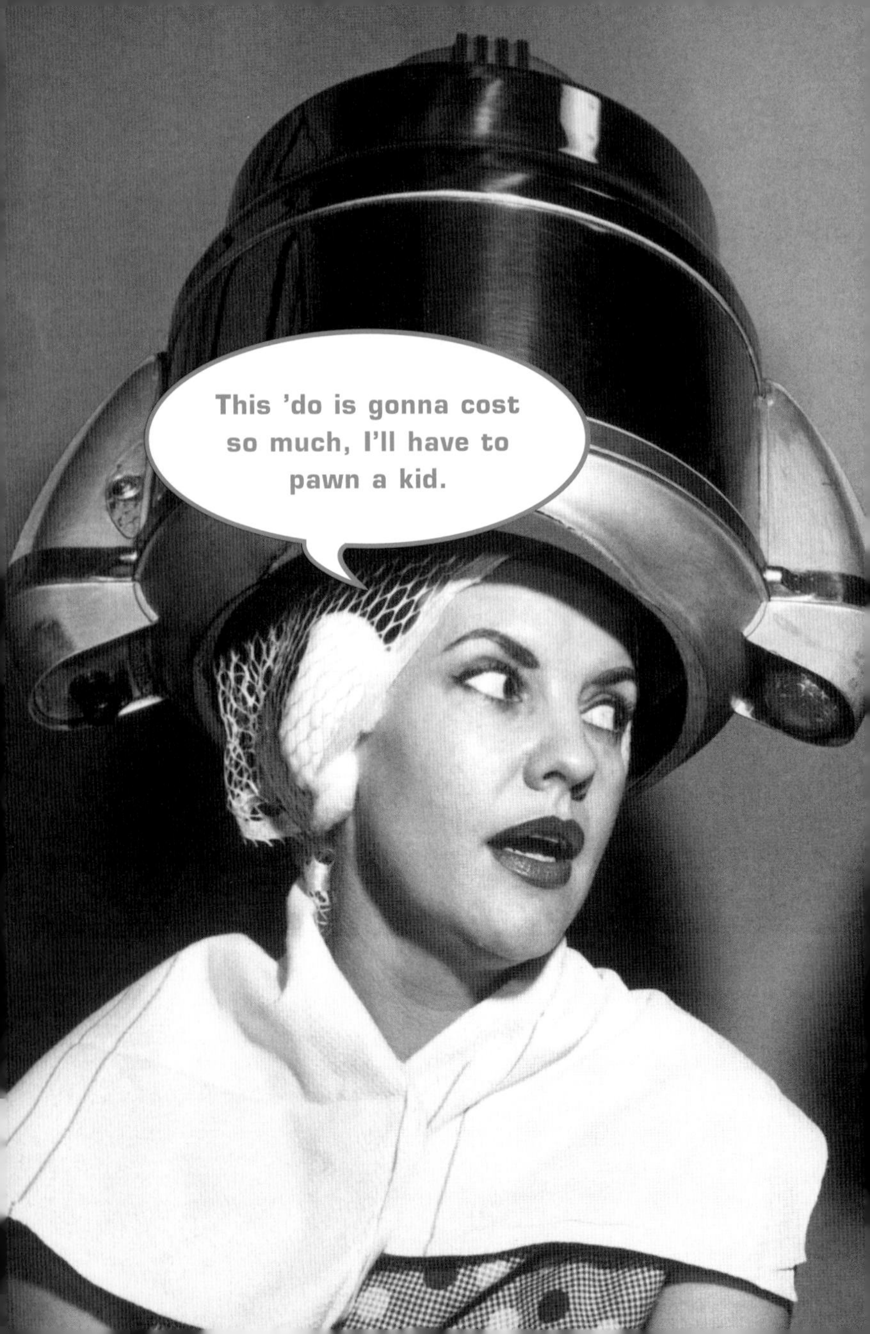
This 'do is gonna cost so much, I'll have to pawn a kid.

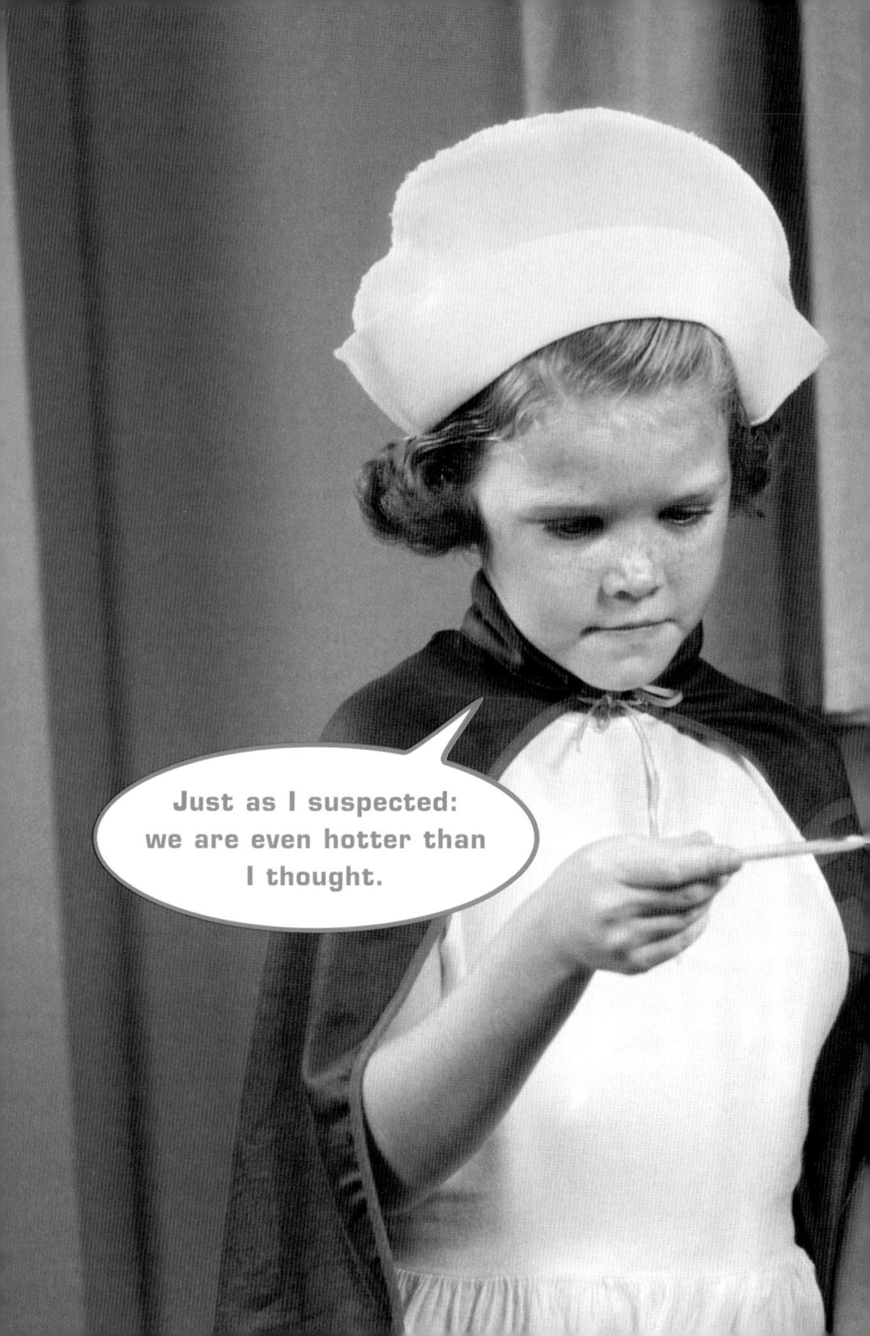
Just as I suspected: we are even hotter than I thought.

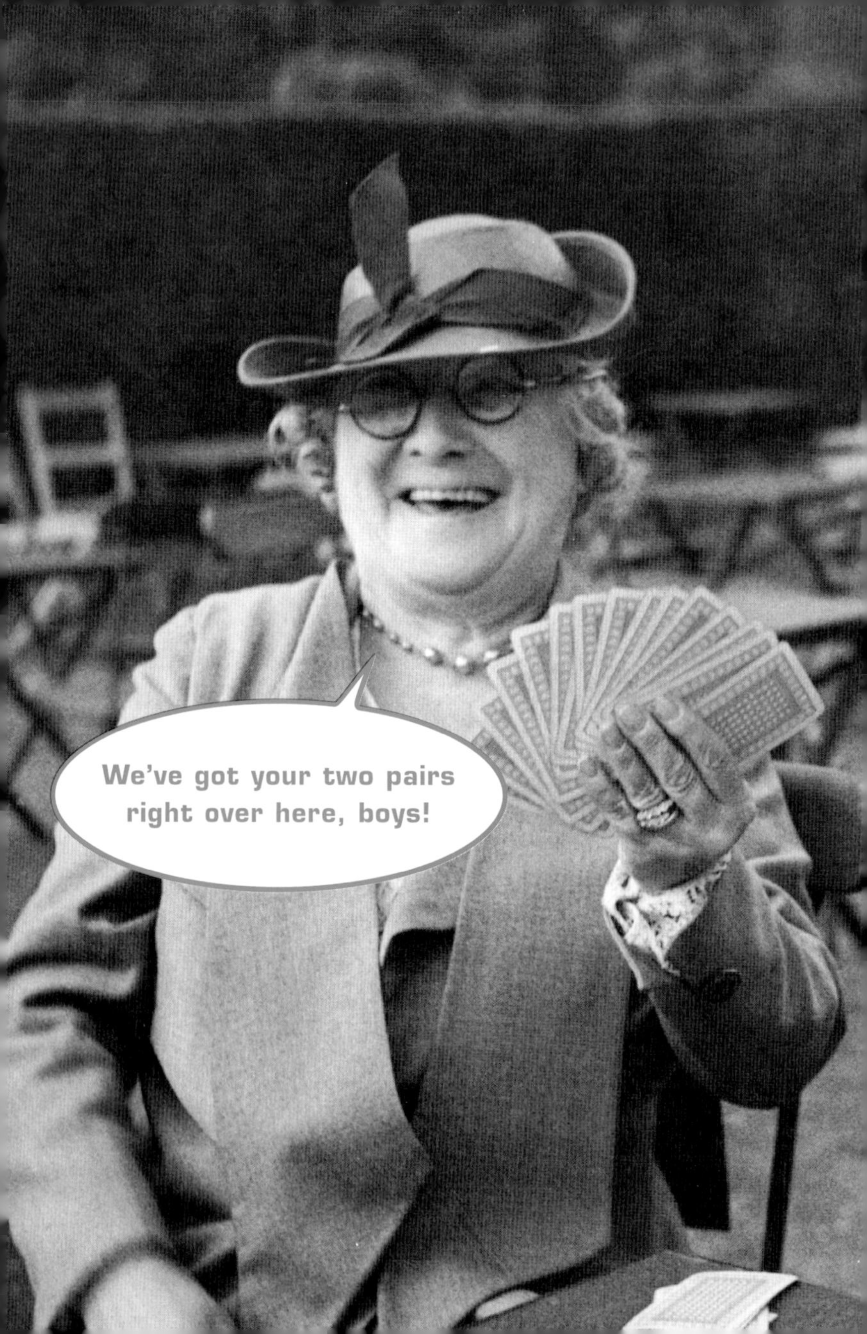
We've got your two pairs
right over here, boys!

A Girl
NEEDS FRIENDS WITH
FUZZY MATH SKILLS.

~

REPAIRS
Ooooh.
Two thousand calories times twelve cakes. That's only like ten minutes on the treadmill.
FOR CAKE

Barb and Mildred
JUST REMEMBER THEY LEFT
THEIR HUSBANDS AT THE
CONCESSION STAND.

~

Friends
**DON'T LET YOU SWEAT
THE SMALL STUFF.**

~

Let me get this straight.
You say now I get to bring
home the bacon, fry it,
and scrub the pan?

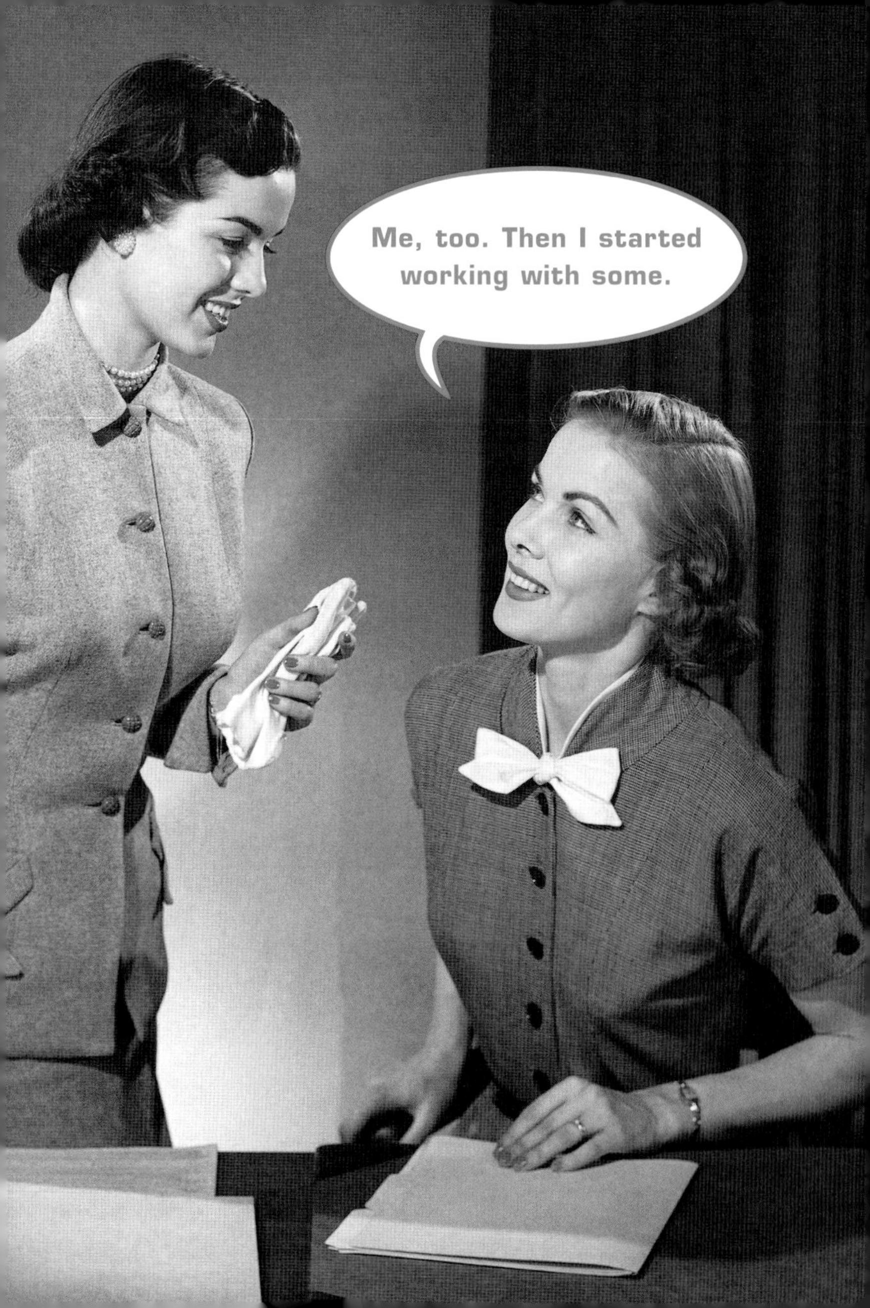
Me, too. Then I started working with some.

It's my new hobby—growing orgasmic vegetables.

The first thing you have to do is lose the braids and get yourself some curls. That's when things really started taking off for me.

So when he's done with the lawn, I'll go clog the sink, and he'll have to come back tomorrow.

Advice
**FROM IDA'S
PERSONAL TRAINER**

~

The trick is to pedal only when a cute guy is watching. Otherwise, save your strength for canasta.

True Friends
WON'T LET YOU SETTLE.

~

Remember the rules:
If it's smaller than six inches,
throw it back.

. . . *And*
THAT WAS THE LAST
TIME THE HOSPITAL
CAFETERIA SERVED TOFU
"MEATBALLS."

~

AIRWAYS LI

Royal Bay

Let's Be
THE KIND OF WOMEN WHO PUT GIRLIE DEODORANTS TO THE TEST!

~

Forget this.
Let's just look helpless and wait to be rescued. You know, like a man in a kitchen.
POOL
NB
KU 317

Look!
They printed my ad! "Free to a good home: One husband, three kids. Will deliver."

Swimsuit Season

TOTALLY BLOWS.

~

Do you remember what happened that night?

Why
THE REALLY GOOD STUFF
NEVER MAKES IT INTO
THE SCRAPBOOK

~

Here's the nickel
my daddy gave me when
I started dating,
in case I needed to call home.
But they were such gentlemen . . .

those bastards.

Joan and Mary ENJOYED SHARING THEIR FRUSTRATIONS OVER LUNCH. EACH ONE TOOK TURNS TYPING UP THE LIST.

~

Ball
IN THE GUTTER: BAD.
MIND IN THE GUTTER:
BETTER.

~

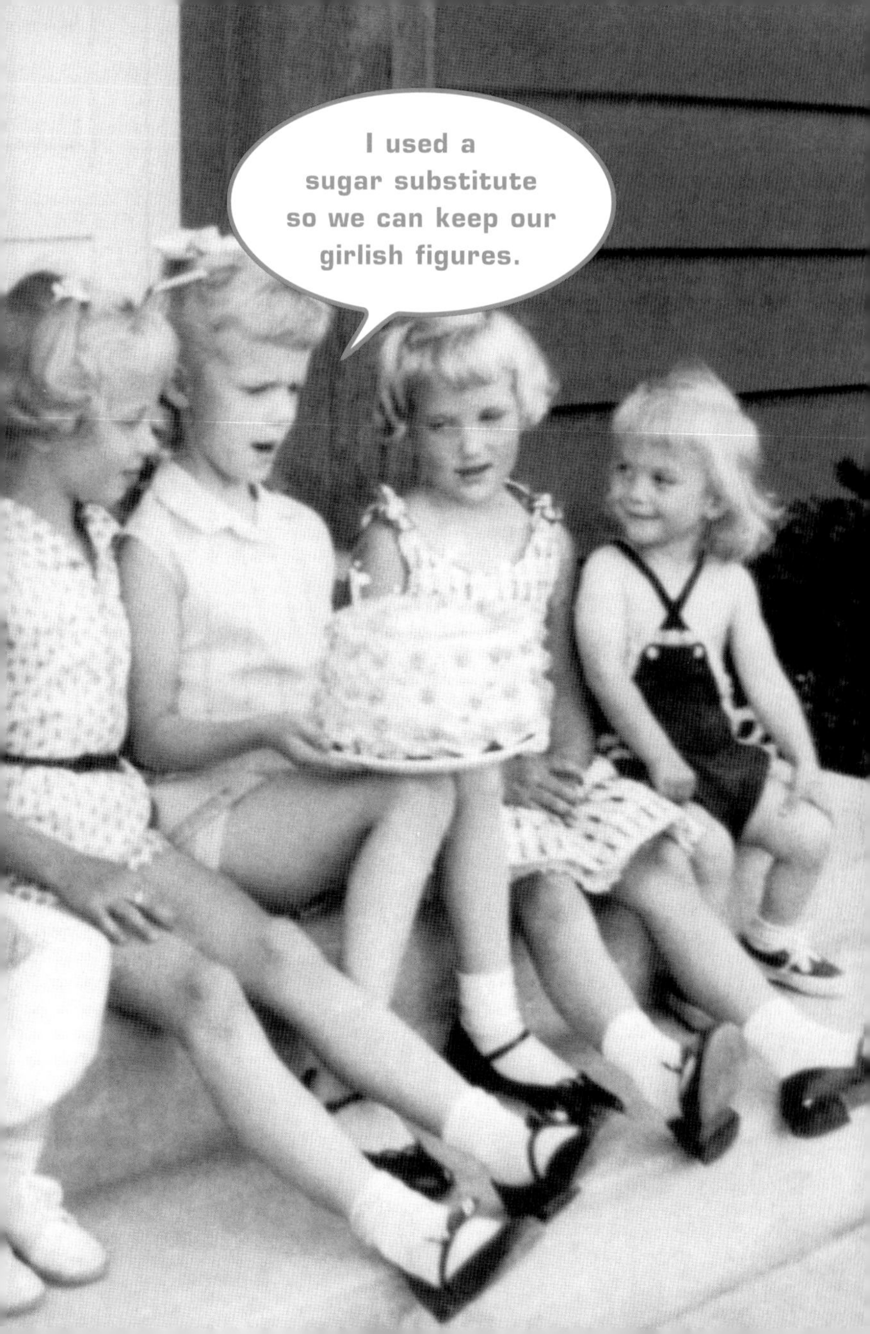
I used a sugar substitute so we can keep our girlish figures.

Ever Notice
BEER GOGGLES WORK
ON YOURSELF, TOO?
AFTER A COUPLE OF
COLD ONES, YOUR BUTT
LOOKS REALLY GOOD
IN THAT BIKINI.

~

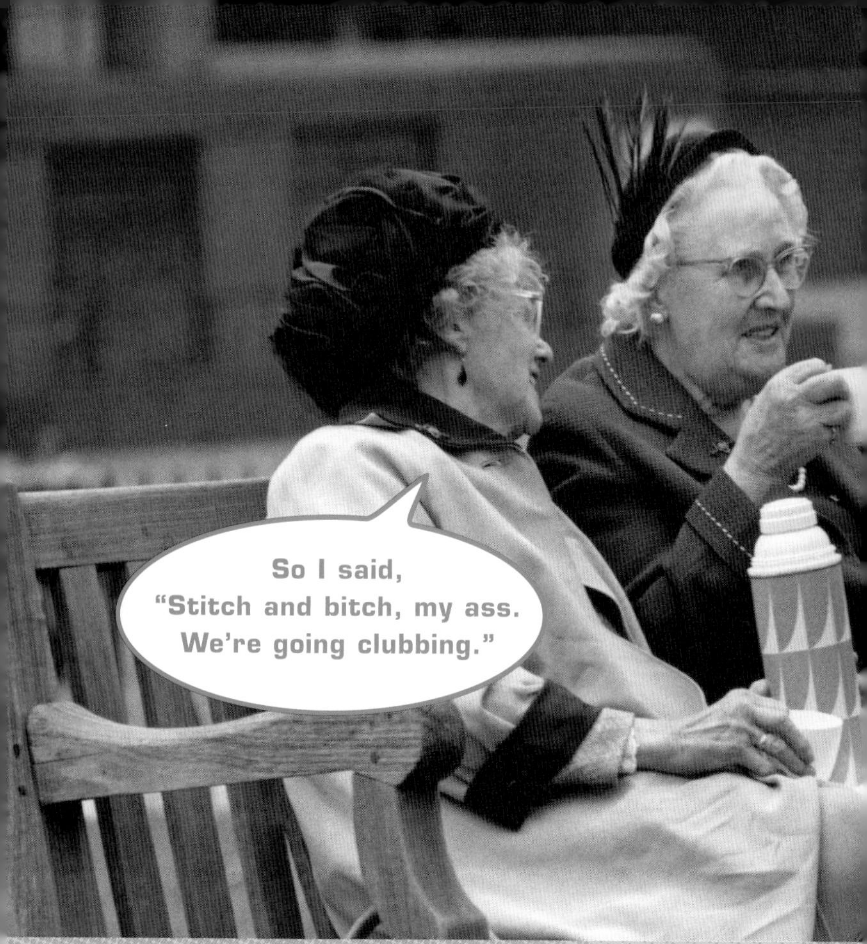
So I said,
"Stitch and bitch, my ass.
We're going clubbing."

In Every Group,
THERE'S ALWAYS A "FUN" ONE.
~

After
YET ANOTHER DATE WITH
A DEGENERATE LOSER,
DARLA DEDICATES HER LIFE
TO PERFECTING THE COSMO.

~

The Best Thing

ABOUT OLD FRIENDS:
THEY'LL TELL YOU
IF YOU'VE GOT SPINACH
IN YOUR TEETH. OR IF
YOU *FORGOT* YOUR TEETH.

~

All I want is
peace on earth . . .
. . . and some really
cute shoes.

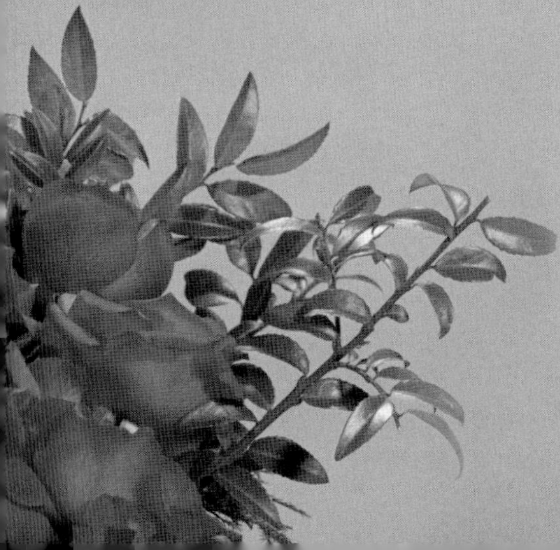

Girls, when you talk,
we listen. If this book
gave you the giggles,
drop us a line.

Please send your comments to:
Book Feedback
2501 McGee, Mail Drop 215
Kansas City, MO 64108

Or e-mail us at
booknotes@hallmark.com